HOW

BIG

IS "YOUR" BIBLE?

Committing Holy Scripture To Memory

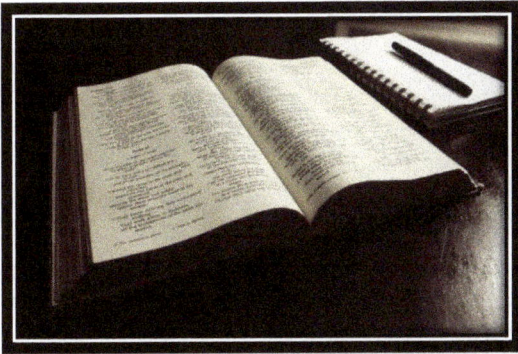

Compiled by *Prophetess Wanda K. Tucker*

Women As Treasure ®

Copyright © 2025

How "BIG" Is Your Bible?: Committing Holy Scripture To Memory

By Prophetess Wanda Tucker

Independently published by Apostle Lance Tucker I

& Nspirational Treasure International, LLC

ISBN: 979-8-9855395-1-6

Binding and Printing: KDP

Book Cover by Nspirational Treasure International, LLC

Forward

One of the most amazing things I can say about Prophetess Wanda Tucker is her love for the Word of God. Ever since I've known her, she has had a tremendous desire to read the Bible. Especially the Old Testament. Man, how she loves those stories. In fact, prior to my salvation, it was Wanda who would read the Bible to me. I was like a little kid, sitting at her knee, listening to those amazing and fantastic stories. She made them come alive for me and caused me to want to know more. She was my first Bible teacher.

As the years went by, she would study to know more and more of what God had to say to His people. And as she filled herself up with the Word, she began to share it with all who would listen. Her Bible was no longer just words on paper, or in a book, but they were living Words of God, coming from her heart. And as the Word says, "hide the Word in your heart, that you don't sin against God."

As a mature Christian Prophetess Wanda would always tell people, "Don't let the Word or your gifting die with you". "When you leave this earth leave empty. Pour into others what the Father has given you to share." And she is right. We shouldn't take it to the grave. We must leave the Life of the Word with the lost.

She is now asking others, "what Word is in you?" "How much Word do you really know?" "How Big is the Bible within you?" We must have the Word of God within us so we can call upon it at all times. For when paper and pen are no long longer available, the Word of God will be in you. You will be able to share it with those who may not have the Word. We must store God's Word within us.

Oh, and another amazing thing about Prophetess Wanda Tucker is this, she is the love of my life. My beautiful wife. And I am so very proud of her for this awesome book. I pray it blesses all who read it.

Apostle Dr. Lance G. Tucker I
LWT Apostolic Ministries

This Book Is Dedicated To...

_____

Place Your Name Here

I Declare that as you consume the written word of God you will be filled to overflowing.

So much so that as "Your" Bible grows within you, you will be able to feed others from the storehouse of your heart...

That according to John 7:38 KJV

"Rivers of living water shall flow from your belly."

In the name of Jesus, Amen.

Prophetess Wanda Tucker

Acknowledgments

Thank you, Apostle Doctor Lance G. Tucker I, you hold many positions in my heart and life. First and foremost, you are my friend, and I love you dearly. You are my husband, my Apostle, the father of our children, my cheerleader, and my eating buddy LOL. Thank you for always having my back.

Thank you to our natural children (and spouses), grands, and great grands for your love. You mean the world to me. To our many spiritual children, thank you for wanting to be part of the Tucker Family.

Love and appreciation to Cynthia and Mama Polite. The Lord used a teenage girl, her faith, her mother's willingness to show love and hospitality to save my life years ago. My love for scripture began in the Polite home, playing Bible Swords and keeping the Sabbath.

A heartfelt thank you to Prophetess Sonya Baker of Power House Christian Fellowship of Auroa Colorado for the opportunity to facilitate the women's portion of their Virtual Vacation Bible School 2024. It was through these sessions that the Lord gave me the thought that led to the writing of this book. Keep pressing forward "Women Of Hope"! The name of your ministry says it all. You express hope to all you encounter.

Thank You Jesus! For it is in and through You that I press towards the mark.

From The Author

Hello dear reader,

I am excited about this opportunity to share the first of what I believe to be several publications. How fitting that this writing is for the most part about the Word of God. Specifically memorizing the Word; John 1:1 tells us "In the beginning was the Word, and the Word was with God, and the Word was God."

As you begin or continue to commit the Word to memory know and understand that Jesus is the Word. Consume Him, allow Him to become part of you. Allow Jesus to make the necessary changes in your heart and mind that will ultimately draw you closer to Him.

Prophetess Wanda Tucker

Contents

Preface

This book is not meant to be sacrilegious. There is but one Bible and that is the Holy Word of God.

"All scripture is given by inspiration of God, and it is profitable for doctrine, reproof, correction, and instruction in righteousness. That the man of God may be perfect, thoroughly furnished unto all good works."
- II Timothy 3: 16,17

Here is the Who, What, When, Where, and Why of this little book.

- o **WHO** – Our Lord and Savior Jesus Christ
- o **WHAT** – The written Word of God
- o **WHEN** – In the beginning was the Word, and the Word was with God, and the Word was God. (John 1:1)

o **WHERE** – Thy Word have I hid in my heart, that I might not sin against thee. (Psalms 119:11)

o **WHY** – This book of the law shall not depart from your mouth, but you shall meditate on it day and night, so that you may be careful to do according to all that is written in it; for then you will make your way prosperous, and then you will have success. (Joshua 1:8)

While recently teaching a Virtual Vacation Bible School class I posed this question to the class. "How big would your Bible be if it only contained the scriptures you had committed to memory?" It was a thought-provoking question that Holy Spirit prompted me to ask. Not only of the participants but for myself as well.

It is all about Jesus, He is the Word of God. If and when we hide Him in our heart, meaning when we commit the Word (Scripture) to memory no one can ever take that away from us.

This is my concern; that the word of God is so accessible, that it is no longer a big book that sits on our coffee tables. There are Bible apps on our laptops, our desktops, and on our phones. The word of God can be read aloud to us by a simple command. Scriptures can be brought to our screens with us only knowing a few words from a particular verse. This should be a good thing! Right?

Technology is a good thing; it can be a great tool when used properly. My prayer is that the convenience of this great tool does not handicap our desire, nor our ability to commit the word of God to **Memory**.

For this reason, I was prompted to compile this book. It is being offered prayerfully to provoke you to '***WRITE***' the word of God upon your heart that you might not sin against Him.

Introduction

How Big Is "YOUR" Bible?

You know, the scriptures you have memorized...

I poised this question to a group of women recently. The premise being that they would be prompted hypothetically to compare the thickness of the sixty-six books contained in the Holy Word of God, with the thickness of their imaginary (or memorized) 'Bible'.

Your 'BIBLE' would only contain scriptures that had been committed to your memory. Hence, the question... **How Big Is Your Bible?**

There are several scriptures and probably many great writings by theologians that expound upon the word of God. Writings that tell of our Heavenly Father's will, and His purpose for us His children. There is a chapter of scripture that sums up the word of God for me, I would like to share it with you. Some no doubt have read it many times before.

The Book of John 1:1-51

1) *In the beginning was the Word, and the Word was with God, and the Word was God.*

2) *He was in the beginning with God.*

3) *All things were made through him, and without him was not anything made that was made.*

4) *In him was life, and the life was the light of men.*

5) *The light shines in the darkness, and the darkness has not overcome it.*

6) *There was a man sent from God, whose name was John.*

7) *He came as a witness, to bear witness about the light, that all might believe through him.*

8) *He was not the light, but came to bear witness about the light.*

9) *The true light, which gives light to everyone, was coming into the world.*

10) *He was in the world, and the world was made through him, yet the world did not know him.*

11) *He came to his own, and his own people did not receive him.*

12) *But to all who did receive him, who believed in his name, he gave the right to become children of God,*

13) *who were born, not of blood nor of the will of the flesh nor of the will of man, but of God.*

14) *And the Word became flesh and dwelt among us, and we have seen his glory, glory as of the only Son from the Father, full of grace and truth.*

15) *(John bore witness about him, and cried out, "This was he of whom I said, 'He who comes after me ranks before me, because he was before me.")*

16) *For from his fullness we have all received, grace upon grace.*

17) *For the law was given through Moses; grace and truth came through Jesus Christ.*

18) *No one has ever seen God; the only God, who is at the Father's side, he has made him known.*

19) *And this is the testimony of John, when the Jews sent priests and Levites from Jerusalem to ask him, "Who are you?"*

20) *He confessed, and did not deny, but confessed, "I am not the Christ."*

21) *And they asked him, "What then? Are you Elijah?" He said, "I am not." "Are you the Prophet?" And he answered, "No."*

22) *So they said to him, "Who are you? We need to give an answer to those who sent us. What do you say about yourself?"*

23) *He said, "I am the voice of one crying out in the wilderness, 'Make straight the way of the Lord,' as the prophet Isaiah said."*

24) *(Now they had been sent from the Pharisees.)*

25) *They asked him, "Then why are you baptizing, if you are neither the Christ, nor Elijah, nor the Prophet?"*

26) *John answered them, "I baptize with water, but among you stands one you do not know,*

27) *even he who comes after me, the strap of whose sandal I am not worthy to untie."*

28) *These things took place in Bethany across the Jordan, where John was baptizing.*

29) *The next day he saw Jesus coming toward him, and said, "Behold, the Lamb of God, who takes away the sin of the world!*

30) *This is he of whom I said, 'After me comes a man who ranks before me, because he was before me.'*

31) *I myself did not know him, but for this purpose I came baptizing with water, that he might be revealed to Israel."*

32) *And John bore witness: "I saw the Spirit descend from heaven like a dove, and it remained on him.*

33) *I myself did not know him, but he who sent me to baptize with water said to me, 'He on whom you see the Spirit descend and remain, this is he who baptizes with the Holy Spirit.'*

34) *And I have seen and have borne witness that this is the Son of God."*

35) *The next day again John was standing with two of his disciples,*

36) *and he looked at Jesus as he walked by and said, "Behold, the Lamb of God!"*

37) *The two disciples heard him say this, and they followed Jesus.*

38) *Jesus turned and saw them following and said to them, "What are you seeking?" And they said to him, "Rabbi" (which means Teacher), "where are you staying?"*

39) *He said to them, "Come and you will see." So they came and saw where he was staying, and they stayed with him that day, for it was about the tenth hour.*

40) *One of the two who heard John speak and followed Jesus was Andrew, Simon Peter's brother.*

41) *He first found his own brother Simon and said to him, "We have found the Messiah" (which means Christ).*

42) *He brought him to Jesus. Jesus looked at him and said, "You are Simon the son of John. You shall be called Cephas" (which means Peter).*

43) *The next day Jesus decided to go to Galilee. He found Philip and said to him, "Follow me."*

44) *Now Philip was from Bethsaida, the city of Andrew and Peter.*

45) *Philip found Nathanael and said to him, "We have found him of whom Moses in the Law and also the prophets wrote, Jesus of Nazareth, the son of Joseph."*

46) *Nathanael said to him, "Can anything good come out of Nazareth?" Philip said to him, "Come and see."*

47) *Jesus saw Nathanael coming toward him and said of him, "Behold, an Israelite indeed, in whom there is no deceit!"*

48) *Nathanael said to him, "How do you know me?" Jesus answered him, "Before Philip called you, when you were under the fig tree, I saw you."*

49) *Nathanael answered him, "Rabbi, you are the Son of God! You are the King of Israel!"*

50) *Jesus answered him, "Because I said to you, 'I saw you under the fig tree,' do you believe? You will see greater things than these."*

51) *And he said to him, "Truly, truly, I say to you, you will see heaven opened, and the angels of God ascending and descending on the Son of Man.*

The Son of Man

Our Lord and Savior Jesus Christ

Memorization

Do you remember taking Spelling Test and memorizing your Multiplication Tables when you were back in grade school? I can remember sitting on the kitchen stool while dinner was being prepared. My Dad would call out one of my spelling words. It would go something like this:

Dad: Neighbor
Me: Neighbor, n, e, i, g, h, b, o, r. Neighbor

I was to pronounce the word, spell the word, and then say the word again. I chose that word because I was far into my adult years before I could spell that word with some type of certainty. It would trip me up every time.

What I did not know was that this type of drill is called Rote or Repetitive Memorization. I had a list of words and I repeated them until they were committed to my memory.

Here are a few other methods to commit scripture to memory. I will first list Rote and its definition.

1) ***Rote**/Repetitive Memorization: Compile a list of all the information you need to remember and rehearse it until it becomes firmly ingrained in your memory.*

2) ***Associative** Memorization Technique: This approach requires constructing a mental journey or visualization linked to the material you aim to remember. In this case associating a scripture with a specific image, individual, or illustration can enhance your memory retrieval.*

3) ***Mnemonics** are memory aids designed to enhance recall. They are prompts or cues and are effective for forming strong long-term memories. For example, T.L.I.M.S. "The Lord Is My Shepherd."*

4) ***Chunking** Technique: Arrange information into manageable groups or categories, then commit each segment to memory systematically.*

5) ***Vocalization*** *Strategy: Research indicates that you are more likely to retain information when you speak it out loud rather than reading it silently.*

Find what works for you, there are many techniques. Understand that nothing will work if you don't try. You must be willing to commit time and effort for any of the techniques to work.

Five Smooth Stones

The David and Goliath story can be found in I Samuel chapter 17. Even though it's a long chapter it is well worth the read. Full disclosure I am partial to the Old Testament stories. It is from this text that I have pulled out the title for this chapter.

You may wonder why David chose to arm himself with five smooth stones, a sling, and his staff. I Samuel 17:40 may make you wonder, with only one Goliath to confront, why the additional equipment? Was the staff a contingency plan in case he missed Goliath with the stones? The Bible does not offer specific reasons for David's choices.

When you read the story, you learn that David in times past used the staff to protect his sheep against predators. However, a staff seems inadequate against a giant with Goliath's might. As for the five smooth stones, why not just one? David spoke with confidence in God's intervention noted in I Samuel 17:47. But we learn that Goliath was not the only one of his kind; when you read, I Chronicles 20:5-8 you learn that he had brothers, and that there were other giants from Gath, Goliath's hometown.

David prepared himself against potential threats from Goliath's brothers or other giants from Gath. Like David, we must anticipate future challenges while trusting God to fight our battles. Know that the enemy will rage and will seem like a giant foe that we have no hope of defeating. We are not in this battle alone, and we are not defenseless!

We are told in Ephesians 6:17 to take the helmet of salvation, and the sword of the Spirit which is the word of God. The Sword is the only offensive weapon listed in our armor. We can fight and win when instructed to do so.

When we face monumental problems, what "five smooth stones" do we need? What five stones or scriptures will you choose? At some point during our lives, we may encounter an insurmountable circumstance. Will we, like David, trust in God's ability to save and protect us?

Read I Samuel 17:47b again. "… For the battle is the Lord's, and he will give you into our hand". Our trust should lie not in our abilities but in God's unwavering support, for "if God is for us, who can be against us" (Romans 8:31).

So, choose your "Five Smooth Stones", your go-to scriptures if you will. Scriptures that will go before you when you must go into battle.

When you have gathered your 'Five Smooth Stones' and have them securely in your pouch, (vs. 40 - in our case we place them in our heart and mind); you can and should Run boldly (vs. 48) into battle. Don't cower in fear or trepidation. Mighty is our God! (Ps. 147:5) The Lord our God goes before us! (Deut. 1:30; .Deut. 9:3).

List your Five Smooth Stones here, your Battle Scriptures

1) _____
   _____
   _____
   _____
   _____
   _____
   _____
   _____
   _____

2) _____
   _____

_____
_____
_____
_____
_____
_____
_____

3) _____
_____
_____
_____
_____
_____
_____
_____

4) _____
_____
_____
_____
_____

_____

_____

_____

5) _____

_____

_____

_____

_____

_____

_____

_____

_____

The Story of David and Goliath - 1 Samuel 17:1-58

*(The **bolded** words were added by me for emphasis)*

1) *Now the Philistines gathered their armies for battle. And they were gathered at Socoh, which belongs to Judah, and encamped between Socoh and Azekah, in Ephes-dammim.*

2) *And Saul and the men of Israel were gathered, and encamped in the Valley of Elah, and drew up in line*

of battle against the Philistines.

3) *And the Philistines stood on the mountain on the one side, and Israel stood on the mountain on the other side, with a valley between them.*

4) *And there came out from the camp of the Philistines a champion named Goliath of Gath, whose height was six cubits and a span.*

5) *He had a helmet of bronze on his head, and he was armed with a coat of mail, and the weight of the coat was five thousand shekels of bronze.*

6) *And he had bronze armor on his legs, and a javelin of bronze slung between his shoulders.*

7) *The shaft of his spear was like a weaver's beam, and his spear's head weighed six hundred shekels of iron. And his shield-bearer went before him.*

8) *He stood and shouted to the ranks of Israel, "Why have you come out to draw up for battle? Am I not a Philistine, and are you not servants of Saul? Choose a man for yourselves, and let him come down to me.*

9) *If he is able to fight with me and kill me, then we will be your servants. But if I prevail against him and kill him, then you shall be our servants and serve us."*

10) *And the Philistine said, "I defy the ranks of Israel this day. Give me a man, that we may fight together."*

11) *When Saul and all Israel heard these words of the Philistine, they were dismayed and greatly afraid.*

12) **Now David was the son of an Ephrathite of Bethlehem in Judah, named Jesse, who had eight sons.** *In the days of Saul the man was already old and advanced in years.*

13) **The three oldest sons of Jesse had followed Saul to the battle.** *And the names of his three sons who went to the battle were Eliab the firstborn, and next to him Abinadab, and the third Shammah.*

14) **David was the youngest.** *The three eldest followed Saul,*

15) *but David went back and forth from Saul to feed his father's sheep at Bethlehem.*

16) *For forty days the Philistine came forward and took his stand, morning and evening.*

17) **And Jesse said to David his son, "Take for your brothers an ephah of this parched grain, and these ten loaves, and carry them quickly to the camp to your brothers.**

18) *Also take these ten cheeses to the commander of their thousand. See if your brothers are well, and bring some token from them."*

19) *Now Saul and they and all the men of Israel were in*

the Valley of Elah, fighting with the Philistines.

20) ***And David rose early in the morning and left the sheep with a keeper and took the provisions and went, as Jesse had commanded him****. And he came to the encampment as the host was going out to the battle line, shouting the war cry.*

21) *And Israel and the Philistines drew up for battle, army against army.*

22) *And David left the things in charge of the keeper of the baggage and ran to the ranks and went and greeted his brothers.*

23) *As he talked with them, behold, the champion, the Philistine of Gath, Goliath by name, came up out of the ranks of the Philistines and spoke the same words as before. And David heard him.*

24) *All the men of Israel, when they saw the man, fled from him and were much afraid.*

25) *And the men of Israel said, "Have you seen this man who has come up? Surely he has come up to defy Israel. And the king will enrich the man who kills him with great riches and will give him his daughter and make his father's house free in Israel."*

26) *And David said to the men who stood by him, "What shall be done for the man who kills this Philistine and*

takes away the reproach from Israel? For who is this uncircumcised Philistine, that he should defy the armies of the living God?"

27) *And the people answered him in the same way, "So shall it be done to the man who kills him."*

28) **Now Eliab his eldest brother heard when he spoke to the men. And Eliab's anger was kindled against David, and he said, "Why have you come down? And with whom have you left those few sheep in the wilderness? I know your presumption and the evil of your heart, for you have come down to see the battle."**

29) *And David said, "What have I done now? Was it not but a word?"*

30) *And he turned away from him toward another, and spoke in the same way, and the people answered him again as before.*

31) *When the words that David spoke were heard, they repeated them before Saul, and he sent for him.*

32) *And David said to Saul, "Let no man's heart fail because of him. Your servant will go and fight with this Philistine."*

33) *And Saul said to David, "You are not able to go against this Philistine to fight with him, for you are*

but a youth, and he has been a man of war from his
youth."

34) But David said to Saul, "Your servant used to keep
sheep for his father. And when there came a lion, or a
bear, and took a lamb from the flock,

35) I went after him and struck him and delivered it out
of his mouth. And if he arose against me, I caught
him by his beard and struck him and killed him.

36) Your servant has struck down both lions and bears,
and this uncircumcised Philistine shall be like one of
them, for he has defied the armies of the living God."

37) **And David said, "The LORD who delivered me from
the paw of the lion and from the paw of the bear
will deliver me from the hand of this Philistine."
And Saul said to David, "Go, and the LORD be with
you!"**

38) **Then Saul clothed David with his armor. He put a
helmet of bronze on his head and clothed him with
a coat of mail,**

39) **and David strapped his sword over his armor. And
he tried in vain to go, for he had not tested them.
Then David said to Saul, "I cannot go with these,
for I have not tested them." So David put them off.**

40) **Then he took his staff in his hand and chose five**

smooth stones from the brook and put them in his shepherd's pouch. His sling was in his hand, and he approached the Philistine.

41) *And the Philistine moved forward and came near to David, with his shield-bearer in front of him.*

42) *And when the Philistine looked and saw David, he disdained him, for he was but a youth, ruddy and handsome in appearance.*

43) *And the Philistine said to David, "Am I a dog, that you come to me with sticks?" And the Philistine cursed David by his gods.*

44) *The Philistine said to David, "Come to me, and I will give your flesh to the birds of the air and to the beasts of the field."*

45) *Then* **David said to the Philistine, "You come to me with a sword and with a spear and with a javelin, but I come to you in the name of the LORD of hosts, the God of the armies of Israel,** *whom you have defied.*

46) *This day the LORD will deliver you into my hand, and I will strike you down and cut off your head. And I will give the dead bodies of the host of the Philistines this day to the birds of the air and to the wild beasts of the earth, that all the earth may know*

that there is a God in Israel,

47) *and that all this assembly may know that the LORD saves not with sword and spear. For the battle is the LORD's, and he will give you into our hand."*

48) *When the Philistine arose and came and drew near to meet David,* **David ran quickly toward the battle line** *to meet the Philistine.*

49) *And* **David put his hand in his bag and took out a stone and slung it and struck the Philistine on his forehead. The stone sank into his forehead, and he fell on his face to the ground**.

50) *So* **David prevailed over the Philistine with a sling and with a stone**, *and struck the Philistine and killed him. There was no sword in the hand of David.*

51) *Then David ran and stood over the Philistine and took his sword and drew it out of its sheath and killed him and cut off his head with it. When the Philistines saw that their champion was dead, they fled.*

52) *And the men of Israel and Judah rose with a shout and pursued the Philistines as far as Gath and the gates of Ekron, so that the wounded Philistines fell on the way from Shaaraim as far as Gath and Ekron.*

53) *And the people of Israel came back from chasing the Philistines, and they plundered their camp.*

54) *And David took the head of the Philistine and brought it to Jerusalem, but he put his armor in his tent.*

55) *As soon as Saul saw David go out against the Philistine, he said to Abner, the commander of the army, "Abner, whose son is this youth?" And Abner said, "As your soul lives, O king, I do not know."*

56) *And the king said, "Inquire whose son the boy is."*

57) *And as soon as David returned from the striking down of the Philistine, Abner took him, and brought him before Saul with the head of the Philistine in his hand.*

58) *And Saul said to him, "Whose son are you, young man?" And David answered, "I am the son of your servant Jesse the Bethlehemite."*

Arrows In My Quiver

A quiver is an archer's portable case for holding arrows. Archery refers to the sport, practice, or expertise of using a bow to launch arrows. Throughout history, archery has served purposes in both hunting and warfare. Arrows are essential for a warrior's success.

Hunting - Genesis 27:3 Mentions hunting with arrows when Isaac tells his son Esau, "Now therefore, please take your weapons, your quiver and your bow, and go out to the field and hunt game for me."

Defense / Warfare - Ephesians 6:16 States, "above all, taking the shield of faith, with which you will be able to quench all the fiery darts of the wicked one." This verse encourages us, as believers, to employ our faith as a shield to protect ourselves from the spiritual attacks of the enemy, represented as flaming arrows. Understand that the enemy has arrows as well. Our faith in Jesus and the word of God can and will protect us.

Offence / Warfare - Psalm 127:4-5 says, "Like arrows in the hands of a warrior, so are the children of one's youth. Blessed is the man who has his quiver is full of them…" This verse compares our children to being arrows in our hands. When we launch our children into society, children that we have raised in the fear and admonition of the Lord; they have the potential of making a big impact on society.

We are warriors, we have the strength and protection of the word of God. Instill the word into your heart and into the hearts of your children. May our quivers ever overflow with scripture as well as with God-fearing children.

So, with the 'quiver' foundation squarely laid let's delve into the arrows that are in your quiver. Metaphorically the arrows are the scriptures that you can use both offensively and defensively. Arrows that you have placed into your quiver; your heart.

When you place a scripture into your heart, you have memorized it. You don't need an app to pull it up. You have the ability to use the greatest 'computer' in the world. Your brain!

In the space below list the scriptures – book, chapter, and verse(s) - that you have committed to memory. (Example: II Chronicles 20:17)

1) _____

2) _____

3) _____

4) _____

5) _____

6) _____

7) _____

8) _____

9) _____

10) _____

11) _____

12) _____

13) _____

14) _____

15) _____

16) _____

17) _____

18) _____

19) _____

20) _____

If those twenty spaces weren't enough to list the 'arrows' in your quiver – Good for You! There will be a few pages at the end of this booklet for you to list more. If the twenty spaces were perhaps nineteen spaces to many… get to work on filling in the spaces. I would like to offer five easy or at least not very challenging scripture to get you started on filling your quiver.

1) *"Thy word is a lamp onto my feet, and a light onto my path." Psalm" 119:105*

2) *"Heaven and earth shall pass away, but my words shall not pass away." Matthew 24:35*

3) *"But be doers of the word, and not hearers only, deceiving yourselves." James 1:22*

4) *"The grass withers. the flower fades, but the word of our God will stand forever." Isaiah 40:8*

5) *"The LORD is my shepherd; I shall not want." Psalm 23:1*

One Bonus, the shortest scripture in the Bible.

6) *"Jesus wept." John 11:35*

Growing "OUR" Bibles

If you skipped the preface at the beginning of this book, I would ask that you circle back and take a few minutes to read it. It explains my reasoning for wanting us to spend time committing scripture to memory. I know there are some of you that probably won't take the time to go back, so here is a snippet of the details.

I am concerned that we depend heavily on our devices, even when it comes to the Word of God. Next time you're in church conduct a mini non-scientific test. What is the percentage of your fellow parishioners that have brought their actual Bibles with them compared to those that are accessing their electronic devices?

Don't get me wrong, I enjoy the luxury of having the scripture read to me as I exercise or wash dishes. I really like being able to speak to my phone and ask it to find a certain scripture for me. Especially when all I can recall is "scripture is profitable for..." Then just like that, it pops up- "All scripture is given by inspiration of God, and is profitable for doctrine, for reproof, for correction, for instruction in righteousness: That the man of God may be perfect, thoroughly furnished unto all good works." 2 Timothy 3:16,17

What will happen if we no longer have internet access? Will that eliminate our ability to access the Word of God? What will happen if, God forbid, our Bibles are outlawed? After all the Word of God is filled with hate-speech, right? Marriage between one man and one woman? Matthew 19:4-6, also, "For they exchanged the truth of God for a lie and worshiped and served the creature rather than the Creator, who is blessed forever. Amen. Romans 1:25

I digress... my point is this, hide the word of God in your heart. No one will ever be able to take it from you. The scripture also tells us to hide the word in our hearts so that we will not sin against the Lord. Below I have suggested a few scriptures for you to consider. My aim is to get you on your way to 'growing' your Bible. If you have been in church for any amount of time, I am sure you have heard at least one or two of them mentioned before.

Following the scriptures there are pages for you to write out the scriptures if you so desire. Or you can create your own list of verses that you would like to commit to memory.

Here are a few suggested scriptures to add to your Bible:

1) *Romans 8:12-14*
2) *Psalm 145:1-3*
3) *Psalm 102:25-27*
4) *Psalm 119:1*
5) *Psalm 73:25-26*
6) *Psalms 51:1-4*
7) *2 Timothy 3:16*
8) *Matthew 4:4*
9) *Matthew 3:16-17*
10) *John 3:16*
11) *Nehemiah 9:6*
12) *Romans 8:28*
13) *Hebrews 2:3-4*
14) *Hebrews 4:14-16*
15) *Revelation 5:11-12*
16) *James 4:7-8*

17) *Genesis 1:26-27*

18) *Colossians 3:18-19*

19) *Hebrews 8:10*

20) *Romans 3:23-26*

21) *1 Corinthians 15:20-23*

22) *Luke 6:35-36*

23) *Ephesians 1:3-6*

24) *Matthew 11:28-30*

25) *Romans 8:14-17*

26) *John 3:5-8*

27) *Romans 3:27-28*

28) *Romans 6:11-14*

29) *1 Corinthians 12:12-13*

30) *John 10:27-28*

31) *Philippians 1:20-24*

32) *1 Corinthians 15:42-44*

33) *Galatians 2:20*

34) *Psalm 23:1-6*

35) *Isaiah 40:31*

In Closing

Written 5-31-24   10:16am

What difference does it make how big your Bible is if you do not apply it to your life? I can memorize the entire Bible, all 66 books of the Holy Word of God, and yet, if I do not apply even one Scripture to my life, it is of no value. What do I mean by this?

Yesterday I read a devotion. The title of it was *Power of the Sword*. The devotion was a timely read because on the previous day I had submitted much of this book to my publisher. As you have seen this book is all about encouraging you, the reader, to memorize scriptures.

In this devotion, the author was describing a gentleman that had a personal battle with anger. The story became very personal to me. I do not have a battle with anger. My battle is with food. My goal is to eat to live not live to eat. I eat when I'm happy. I eat when I'm sad. I eat when I'm upset. I eat when I watch TV/movies. I enjoy eating on road trips. It probably would be easier for me to just say I love to eat.

This is not so much a problem when you're in your 20s, you enjoy working outside in the yard and you're very active. But as you start to get older, your metabolism starts to slow down. Your body does not process food the same way it used to. You do not burn fat quite as easily. Aside from the vanity portion of it, this could become unhealthy and can even become dangerous. So, I either need to end this love affair with junk food or resign myself to taking medications to ward off certain diseases.

Now, why did I bring up the devotion and the gentleman that had the battle with anger? I'm glad you asked. Now I can stop my narrative and get back to the point at hand. It was not until the gentleman made a covenant with God, which included memorizing and meditating on Colossians 3:8 ("You yourselves, are to put off all these: anger, wrath…"). It was then that the gentleman began to move towards getting a handle on his situation.

You see it was not just the simple point of memorizing a scripture. The gentleman needed to find a scripture that applied specifically to his battle. He didn't need to just memorize it. He needed to apply the scripture to his situation, his battle. Whenever he got angry, he was to rehearse it in his mind. He was to quote the scripture, speak it to himself. It was then the anger began to loosen its grip on his emotions. He asked the Lord to bring the scripture to his mind, whenever he was tempted to lose his temper. The scripture that he memorized then became a sword that he was able to use when he was in the mist of his battle.

Hebrews 4:12 (ESV) states: *"For the word of God is living and active, sharper than any two-edged sword, piercing to the division of soul and of spirit, of joints and of marrow, and discerning the thoughts and intentions of the heart."*

What was it that Jesus did when he was confronted and tempted in the wilderness for 40 days and 40 nights by Satan? When Jesus found Himself in this battle, he decisively quoted the appropriate scripture for His situation. In the book of Matthew chapter 4, verses 1-11 Jesus was quoting from Deuteronomy 8:3 (NKJV), *"So He humbled you, allowed you to hunger, and fed you with manna which you did not know nor did your fathers know, that He might make you know that man shall not live by bread alone; but man, lives by every word that proceeds from the mouth of the Lord."*

So, for my situation, I found three scriptures that I can memorize, meditate on, and apply (quote) when my flesh is trying to be in control. I will also pray and ask Holy Spirit to bring these scriptures to my mind when I am tempted to gratify my flesh with food.

1) <u>*Romans 13:14*</u> - *But put on the Lord Jesus Christ, and make no provision for the flesh, to gratify its desires.*

2) <u>*1 Corinthians 6:19-20*</u> - *Or do you not know that your body is a temple of the Holy Spirit within you, whom you have from God? You are not your own, for you were bought with a price. So glorify God in your body.*

3) <u>*1 Corinthians 3:16-17*</u> - *Do you not know that you are God's temple and that God's Spirit dwells in you? If anyone destroys God's temple, God will destroy him. For God's temple is holy, and you are that temple.*

With this said, I encourage you to continue to grow your Bible. Continue to memorize the word of God. Be the living epistle the world is in desperate need of. I love the quote… "Preach the Gospel at all times. And if necessary, use words." Understand that there is power in the word of God. Your "Big Bible" is not to be for show.

What battle do you find yourself in today? Pull arrows from your quiver, select your five smooth stones. Fight back! Your memorized scriptures will not help you if you do not utilize them. They will be as useful as that big black family Bible that sits on the coffee table with the dust on top of it.

Even though it has been inferred many times within these pages, I want to drive the point home yet again. Memorize your scripture. Meditate on those scripture. Use the scripture, the living Word of God as it was meant to be, the Sword of the Spirit.

I've mentioned before that the word of God is the only offensive portion of your armor that you are to put on daily (Ephesians 6:10-18)? Till we all come in the unity of the faith, and the knowledge of the Son of God…

My prayer is that you will endeavor to increase the size of "Your Bible". More importantly that you will not be satisfied with simply having the ability to quote the Word of God. Study the Word of God so that you will have the ability to obey it!

Remember II Timothy 2:15.

You may be the only Bible someone may ever read. My prayer is that "Your Bible" will continue to increase until He returns! Give them The Good Book. Give them Jesus! **Jesus is the WORD OF GOD.**

Increase My Bible

Journal Pages

On the following pages, record your thoughts regarding the increasing of "your" Bible. The first few have journals prompts for you to consider and the rest are for you to jot down anything that you feel is relevant to help you along this journey of remembrance.

Journal Pages

Why is it important to increase the size of "my" Bible? Why is it of importance to me?

_____

_____

_____

_____

_____

_____

_____

_____

_____

_____

_____

_____

_____

_____

_____

_____

_____

_____

_____

_____

Journal Pages

What scriptures will I turn to when I am feeling sad or discouraged. Why do I find comfort in these scriptures?

_____

_____

_____

_____

_____

_____

_____

_____

_____

_____

_____

_____

_____

_____

_____

_____

_____

_____

_____

Journal Pages

Matthew 28:19-20 gives us a command. How will increasing "my" Bible help me to carry out the instructions of these verses?

_____

_____

_____

_____

_____

_____

_____

_____

_____

_____

_____

_____

_____

_____

_____

_____

_____

_____

Journal Pages

_____

_____

_____

_____

_____

_____

_____

_____

_____

_____

_____

_____

_____

_____

_____

_____

_____

_____

_____

_____

_____

_____

Journal Pages

Treasure Cards

What are they? Good old fashioned flash cards to help you grow "your" Bible.

Added here on the next few pages are sample Treasure Cards to assist you on the journey of increasing the size of your Bible.

Treasure Cards

"Trust in the LORD with all thine heart;
And lean not unto thine own understanding.
In all thy ways acknowledge him, And he
shall direct thy paths."

Treasure Cards

"The LORD is my shepherd; I shall not want. He maketh
me to lie down in green pastures: He leadeth me beside the
still waters. He restoreth my soul: He leadeth me in the
paths of righteousness for his name's sake. Yea, though I
walk through the valley of the shadow of death, I will fear
no evil: for thou art with me; Thy rod and thy staff they
comfort me. Thou preparest a table before me in the
presence of mine enemies: Thou anointest my head with oil;
my cup runneth over. Surely goodness and mercy shall
follow me all the days of my life: And I will dwell in the
house of the LORD for ever."

Treasure Cards

Jeremiah 29:11
(NKJV)

www.womenastreasure.com

Treasure Cards

www.womenastreasure.com

Matthew 6:9-13
(KJV)

Treasure Cards

"For I know the thoughts that I think toward you, says the Lord, thoughts of peace and not of evil, to give you a future and a hope."

Treasure Cards

"After this manner therefore pray ye: Our Father which art in heaven, Hallowed be thy name. Thy kingdom come. Thy will be done in earth, as it is in heaven. Give us this day our daily bread. And forgive us our debts, as we forgive our debtors. And lead us not into temptation, but deliver us from evil: For thine is the kingdom, and the power, and the glory, for ever. Amen."

Treasure Cards

John 3:16
(KJV)

www.womenastreasure.com

Treasure Cards

www.womenastreasure.com

Ephesians 6:10-18
(KJV)

Treasure Cards

"For God so loved the world, that he gave his only begotten Son, that whosoever believeth in him should not perish, but have everlasting life."

Treasure Cards

"Finally, my brethren, be strong in the Lord, and in the power of his might. Put on the whole armour of God, that ye may be able to stand against the wiles of the devil. For we wrestle not against flesh and blood, but against principalities, against powers, against the rulers of the darkness of this world, against spiritual wickedness in high places. Wherefore take unto you the whole armour of God, that ye may be able to withstand in the evil day, and having done all, to stand. Stand therefore, having your loins girt about with truth, and having on the breastplate of righteousness; and your feet shod with the preparation of the gospel of peace; above all, taking the shield of faith, wherewith ye shall be able to quench all the fiery darts of the wicked. And take the helmet of salvation, and the sword of the Spirit, which is the word of God: praying always with all prayer and supplication in the Spirit, and watching thereunto with all perseverance and supplication for all saints."

Treasure Cards

Romans 12:2

(KJV)

www.womenastreasure.com

Treasure Cards

www.womenastreasure.com

Romans 10:9-11

(KJV)

Treasure Cards

"And be not conformed to this world: but be ye transformed by the renewing of your mind, that ye may prove what is that good, and acceptable, and perfect, will of God."

Treasure Cards

"...that if thou shalt confess with thy mouth the Lord Jesus, and shalt believe in thine heart that God hath raised him from the dead, thou shalt be saved. For with the heart man believeth unto righteousness; and with the mouth confession is made unto salvation. For the scripture saith, Whosoever believeth on him shall not be ashamed."

Resources

Women As Treasure ® will be offering Treasure Cards for purchase to assist you on your journey towards increase.

For additional information visit:
www.womenastreasure.com/events

About The Author

Mrs. Wanda Tucker... looking at me now does not reflect my onerous beginnings. As I sat writing these first few lines, a song from my choir days popped into my head. I remember it being sung by James Cleveland.

"He took me and made something beautiful out of my life. He took me and made something beautiful out of my life. Well, He took a wretch, a wretch like me and showed His love and concern. And by His grace He changed my life into a better one. I owe Him my all, I cannot let Him down, cause He's the one who made something beautiful out of my life."

The chorus from this song sums up my feelings regarding my life. Today I can say that I am a daughter of the most high God, a wife of 46 years to the love of my life, a mother, grandmother, great-grand mother, a sister, and an encourager. I have been ordained as a Pastor and a Prophet along with a few other accomplishments to date:

- Diploma - Master of Divinity - United Fellowship Ministries Bible College
- Diploma - School of Prophets /Prophetess Collen Boyd - United Fellowship Ministries Bible College
- Founder and CEO - Women As Treasure ®
- Co-Founder – L.W.T. Apostolic Ministries

By the grace of God, I am blessed to hold different titles. From my youth the only letters I coveted to precede my name were M. R. S. My aspirations as a child were to be a wife and mother. Jesus has blessed me with so much more, I am indeed a blessed woman. I have been married to my beloved husband, Apostle Doctor Lance Tucker I, for forty-six years. I credit my growth to the unwavering support of my husband, our children, and my steadfast faith in Jesus.

My spiritual journey began at the tender age of ten. That was the first time I accepted Jesus into my heart and was water baptized. It was the beginning of my lifelong quest to deepen my relationship with Jesus.

My profound encounter with Holy Spirit happened during the time my husband was stationed in Korea. He was in the Army, and it was not a command sponsored tour. Which simply meant I had no business over there. We believe it was the Lord's plan for me to join my husband in Korea. It was the best thing that could have ever happened to us. We were totally emersed into the word of God. Talk about not forsaking the assembling of ourselves together… there was something going on at Church or Bible study seven days a week.

We were blessed to receive a firm foundation in Kingdom teaching when we returned to the states. Our Bishop, the late Timothy L. Witcher started teaching 'Kingdom' in the early 70's. We stayed with his ministry for thirty-seven years. The Tucker family will forever be grateful for the love, training, and wisdom we received from Bishop Timothy and Luella Witcher.

My desire moving forward is to exemplify a loving Christ centered marriage. (Titus 2:3-5) I desire to herald the Good News of Jesus and His ability to comfort and give deliverance from things that bind women naturally, emotionally and spiritually. (Isaiah 61:1-3) With the Word of God as my example, I remain committed to share love, practical life lessons and inspirational writings, both in word and deed. (I John 4:7) All by the grace and guidance of our Lord Jesus Christ. I am a branch of the Love of God. (John 15:1-5)

I trust you will be blessed by the contents of this book, and that you will strive daily to grow your Bible. As a result of that growth, I am praying that your walk and your faith in God will increase.

May God Richly Bless You and Yours!
Prophetess Wanda Tucker

<u>References</u>

Preface

i.   II Timothy 3:16,17 KJV

ii.   John 1:1 ESV

iii. Psalm 119:11 KJV

iv.   Joshua 1:8 ESV

Introduction

v.   John 1:1-51 ESV

Memorization

vi.   1-4 wikihow.com/memorization-quickly

Five Smooth Stones

vii.   I Samuel 17 ESV

viii. I Samuel 17:40 ESV

ix.   I Samuel 17:47 ESV

x.   I Chronicles 20:5-8 ESV

xi.   Ephesians 6:17 KJV

xii.   I Samuel 17:47b KJV

xiii. Romans 8:31 KJV

xiv.   I Samuel 17:1-58 ESV

Arrows In My Quiver

Growing "Our Bibles"

In Closing